⊖ AN OBS

Making Clot

Fine Finishing

Toni Naldrett

Illustrations by Coral Mula

FREDERICK WARNE

Published by Frederick Warne (Publishers) Ltd, London, 1984

Imperial and metric measurements are used throughout the book.
Choose either the metric or imperial system and stick to it throughout
the project—changing from one system to the other will lead to
inaccuracy and mistakes.

ISBN o 7232 3237 7

Filmset and printed in Great Britain
by BAS Printers Limited, Over Wallop, Hampshire

Contents

Thread and needle guide

The following chart is a guide to choosing the correct needle and thread for your fabric. There are too many individual materials to name, so a few have been given to help identify the weight of your own fabric.

Natural fibres	Machine needle	Thread
Lightweights: crêpes, lawns, wools, silks, cottons	*Sharp*: 11/80 to 14/90	fine, mercerized cotton or pure silk (for silk)
Medium weights: suitings cords, velvets, gaberdines, linens, cottons	14/90	mercerized cotton no 50
Heavyweights: coatings, linen union, denim, sailcloth	16/100	mercerized cotton no 40
Synthetic fibres *Lightweights*: nets, sheers, lingerie fabrics, knits	*Ball point*: 9/70 to 11/80	Synthetic thread, (these are all about the same size)
Medium weights: double knits, polyester jerseys, heavy nylons, stretch knits, polyester sheetings	11/80 to 14/90	synthetic thread
Heavyweights: bonded knits	16/100	synthetic thread
Leather	*Wedge shaped*: 11/80 to 14/90	mercerized cotton no 50 or no 40
PVC	*Sharp*: 16/100	,,
Button-holes and top-stitching For *all* fabrics	Same needle as rest of project	polyester button-hole thread, or double the thread in use

Introduction

This book contains everything you need to know about completing your sewing projects—the final phase of making a garment—when the machining is almost done and the fit is perfect. Now you have to take up the hem, sew the button-holes and put in the zip. You may want to decorate it with trimming or an appliqué design. Don't spoil your work by giving it an untidy and unprofessional finish. Here are tips and techniques to complete your project beautifully and creatively.

Most of the methods shown in this book can be done either on your sewing machine or by hand. Both are correct and it is really up to you which way you choose.

Machine sewing

The modern dressmaker usually needs speedy processes to help her complete her project. The sewing machine will sew everything neatly and strongly, making clothes that stand up to the rigours of daily life and the washing machine. Many dress patterns are now designed to eliminate hand sewing completely, so it pays to learn to use your sewing machine to the full.

BASIC TIPS FOR MACHINE SEWING (Figures 1, 2, 3)

1 Choose the right machine needle for the fabric. Sharp, pointed needles are best for natural fibres and ball-point needles for synthetic fibres. Always start a new project with a new needle, as blunt or jagged needles will cause problems.

2 Choose the correct thread for the fabric. Mercerized cotton is best for natural fibres while synthetic fibres require 100 per cent polyester or Terylene (see the chart on page 4 for information).

3 When threading your machine before sewing, be certain to draw up the bobbin thread by turning the hand-wheel one revolution, then lay both needle and bobbin threads neatly under and behind the foot. Muddled threads can easily knot and choke the start of a seam. Before lowering the foot to begin sewing *always* check that the threads lie this way.

4 Start stitching 12 mm ($\frac{1}{2}$ in) in from the edge, reverse stitch to the edge then proceed forwards until the seam or dart is complete. Reverse 12 mm ($\frac{1}{2}$ in) to finish off.

5 Tacking is not necessary. Hold the seam by pinning horizontally across the stitching line; the machine foot and needle will run over the pins without breaking.

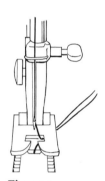

Figure 1

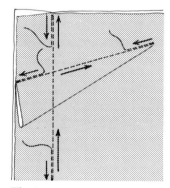

Figure 2

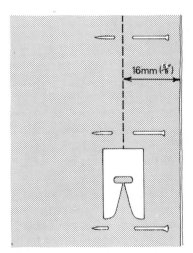

Figure 3

Hand sewing

Nothing gives greater satisfaction to the eye, not to mention the soul, of a dressmaker than a piece of beautiful hand sewing—an invisible hem or a neat button-hole. Before the invention of the sewing machine all clothes were made by hand, taking ages in construction and resulting in real craftsmanship. If you enjoy the peaceful occupation of sewing by hand to finish off your projects your reward will be twofold: a welcome therapy to the hectic pace of life and keeping up high standards of craftsmanship.

BASIC TIPS FOR HAND SEWING

1 Choose the best hand-sewing needle for the fabric. Fine needles are good for all hand-sewing projects. As with the sewing machine, use a sharp pointed needle for natural fibres and a ball-point needle for synthetics.

2 Again, use the right thread for the fabric. See **2** of 'Basic tips for machine sewing'.

3 Do not sew with very long threads; they will tangle and knot, which is infuriating! Cut a thread about 46 cm (18 in) to prevent trouble. It is much easier to thread a needle with a freshly cut thread, so always trim away whiskers of thread.

Chapter 1
Fastening it together

Many dressmakers avoid designs with traditional fastenings like zips and buttons because they consider them too complicated or that they look amateur when finished. This chapter gives tips and techniques for every possible method of fastening your project, so banish the deceitful tricks of snap fasteners lurking beneath buttons.

Buttons and button-holes

CHOOSING BUTTONS

Think carefully about the finished look of your project when choosing the buttons. The best advice is 'simple but good'. Fancy buttons can appear to gild the perfect lily of your project and distract the eye from other more important design details. Cheap plastic or metal buttons can also ruin the finished look. Explore the possibilities of antique buttons and buckles. Use real mother-of-pearl shirt buttons, bone or horn tailor's buttons for elegant simplicity. Antique shops and market stalls, even jumble sales are rich treasure troves for special finds. If all else fails and the buttons or buckles available to you are not the right colour match or size, you can cover purchased moulds in matching fabric.

BUTTON-HOLE THREAD

Button-holes, like other forms of openings on garments, are subject to more wear and tear than the rest of the garment. To counteract this strain special thread, such as button-hole twist and linen thread, can be used. These are thicker and stronger than normal thread and sew a heavy button-hole. Such a heavy button-hole can look out of place on a light blouse or dress, so it is best used on garments designed for heavy duty or an extra long life. The thread works equally well on machined and hand-stitched button-holes. On normal clothing the same no 50 thread you use for all stitching will be more than adequate for button-holes.

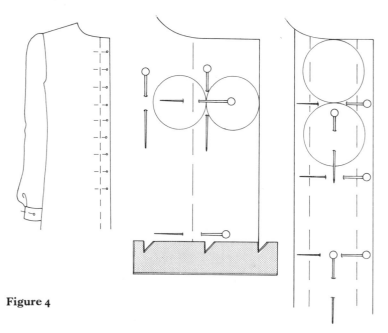

Figure 4

POSITIONING HORIZONTAL BUTTON-HOLES (Figure 4)

Button-holes are usually worked at right angles to the garment edge. Vertical button-holes are described on page 10.

It is really useless to begin making the button-hole without the buttons you intend to use. Hence the advisability of purchasing all the accessories needed for your project at the same time as the fabric and paper pattern. The following instructions are for button-holes on a garment, but the method applies to all kinds of button and button-hole placement.

1 Mark the centre-front line on your garment, if not already done, with a line of French (tailor's) chalk or large tacking stitches.
2 Lay the garment on a flat surface and arrange all the buttons required to make a neat closure. Make sure the distance between each button is equal, measuring from button centre to button centre. Take time and trouble over positioning your buttons as they will be a dominant feature, especially down the centre front of a garment.

3 Pin-mark the final position of your buttons on the centre line. Now place a button between the garment edge and the centre-front line as shown and pin-mark the edge of the button nearest the centre-front line. This will be one end of the button-hole. This simple method ensures that the button will sit neatly inside the button-hole and not slide over the outer edge of the garment—a very amateur mistake.

4 To find the other end of the finished button-hole, place the button against the first pin and mark off with another pin a point 3 mm ($\frac{1}{8}$ in) beyond the button edge. The extra 3 mm ($\frac{1}{8}$ in) is needed to ease the button in and out of the hole.

5 Repeat the process for each button. For speed mark off the points on a piece of paper from the first button and then continue to mark the rest from this gauge.

Positioning vertical button-holes

Some garments, such as shirts, have narrow stitched bands down the front which do not have enough space to place horizontal button-holes. The openings therefore must be vertical.

1 Position the buttons as before and mark the centre of the button on the garment.

2 Repeat the measurement described in **3** in the last paragraph beginning with the top button nearest the neckline or at the point chosen for the top button.

3 Repeat **4** from the last paragraph.

4 Mark on a piece of paper the length of this first button-hole and then use the gauge to mark the other button-holes. Make sure the central button mark is in the centre of the button gauge before marking the button-hole length.

Machine-stitched button-holes

You do need to practise this particular machining process to achieve perfection. But like swimming, once learnt it's never forgotten, so the time and effort spent will be more than repaid in the speedy professional way you can complete your dressmaking projects. All swing-needle (zig zag) machines will do button-holes, and as each machine has a different method you should refer to your instruction book for the method and PRACTISE.

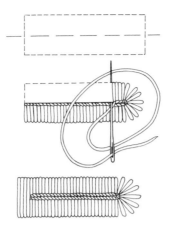

Figure 5

HAND-STITCHED BUTTON-HOLES (Figure 5)

These button-holes are best sewn as one of the last steps in finishing off your project. Button-hole twist or pure silk thread will give a glossy sheen to hand-worked button-holes which greatly enhances the finished work. If your thread becomes twisted during stitching, draw it across a small block of tailor's beeswax.

1 Mark the positions of your button-holes (see page 9).
2 Machine stitch a rectangle around the button-hole to secure the fabric layers, and split open the required length of the button-hole.
3 Stitch (Figure 5) using the machine stitches as a guide.
4 A simple over-and-over stitch is used to make the bar tack. For extra strength, button-hole stitch over the bar tack.
5 Press.

BOUND BUTTON-HOLES (Figure 6)

These lovely button-holes seem to have lost favour and are rarely seen on shop bought garments, except the most expensive couture clothes. The button-hole can become a feature of your garment by using a contrasting fabric, suede or leather for the binding. There are many ways of making bound button-holes but they all need care to ensure accuracy. The method shown is simple. Follow the instructions to add a touch of elegance to your suits and coats.

11

1 Plan to do these button-holes near the beginning of constructing your garment, after attaching the interfacing to the wrong side of the surface on which the button-holes will be sewn. You will find it easier to concentrate on making the button-holes if the area is flat and uncluttered by bits and pieces of collars and sleeves.

2 Working on the wrong side of the garment, position and mark the button-holes as described on p. 9. You can use a pencil to mark positions on the interfacing which will help the accuracy of stitching later on.

3 Draw a rectangle on the interfacing around the button-hole mark, the width of the button-hole being not less than 6 mm ($\frac{1}{4}$ in). Each different button needs individual consideration to make a button-hole to fit, but beware of making the rectangle too deep as it could look bulky when complete. A depth of 6 mm ($\frac{1}{4}$ in) finishes as a neat button-hole shape. Pin the centre of rectangle through all the layers of fabric.

4 Cut patches of self or contrasting fabric either on the straight or bias grain. The patches should measure 7 cm ($2\frac{1}{2}$ in) by 5 cm (2 in). Pin the patches on to the garment, *right sides* together, placing the patches exactly centrally over the centre pin marker. Remove the centre pin marker.

5 Machine stitch round the rectangle as shown, using a smaller stitch for extra strength. Begin stitching away from a corner; this will also strengthen the work.

6 Clip through all the layers as shown, using really *sharp* small pointed scissors to reach the corners. A razor blade or blunt scissors can result in accidents.

7 Unpin the patches and pull the fabric through to the wrong side. Press the rectangle open.

8 Mark half the depth of the rectangle with a pin and fold half the patch to meet the pin. Press again to hold, and fold up the other side, to make the sides meet at the centre. Press again.

9 Slip-stitch the folds to the tiny triangle of fabric underneath at each end of the button-hole.

10 When the rest of the garment has been constructed, carefully pin the facing into position over the button-hole on the inside of the garment. Clip another rectangle through the facing and turn under the edges and slip-stitch to the folded button-hole beneath.

11 Press.

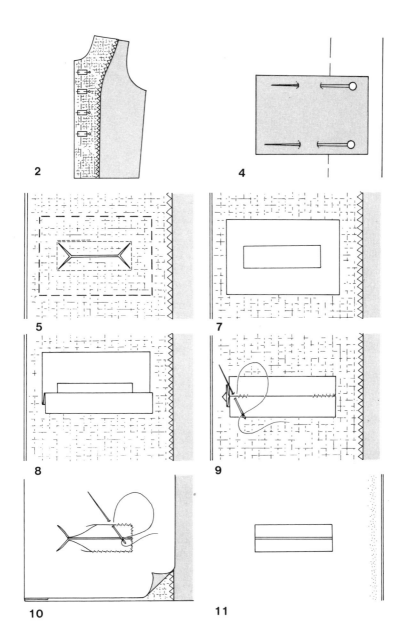

Figure 6

Numbers correspond with those for the written instructions (p. 12).

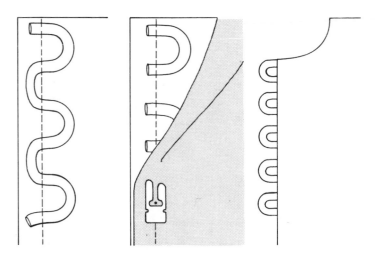

Figure 7

Loop button-holes (Figure 7)

This design of button-hole is shown to its best advantage when used with round ball buttons. They add an old-world charm to blouses and dresses.

Positioning the buttons and button loops

The loop button-hole sits on the edge of the garment, so requires a different technique to measure and position it.

1 Wrap a small scrap of fabric around the ball button and snip the fabric at the two points where it meets. Open out the scrap and the length between the two snips will be the correct length for the loop.

2 Cut narrow strips of fabric on the bias grain. The maximum width of the strip should be 4 cm ($1\frac{3}{4}$ in)—this will finish as a tube of 2 cm ($\frac{3}{4}$ in) circumference.

3 Machine stitch and turn the strip right side out. It helps to stitch across the base of the tube and use the head of a very slim knitting needle to push the tube through.

4 With the garment resting on a flat surface, arrange the buttons and mark the final positions with pins. Remember that the space between buttons must be equal. Ball buttons look best when placed closely side by side.

14

5 Machine stitch the loops as shown, pointing into the garment. Place the loops individually or in a continuous line.

6 Finally, pin and sew the facing on top of the loops, stitching over the first line of sewing. Turn the facing to the wrong side and the loops will fall into the correct position on the edge. Press the edge but take care not to flatten the loops.

Hand-stitched loop button-holes (Figure 8)

1 Position and mark buttons and loops as described.

2 Thread up your needle with button-hole twist or general sewing thread.

3 Use a double thread and, concealing the knot beneath the facing, make a loop through the edge of the garment. Slip the button through the first loop to check for size.

4 Continue to make two or three loops to match and secure with a tiny back-stitch hidden beneath the knot.

5 Button-hole stitch around the loops, holding all the loops within the stitch.

6 Press.

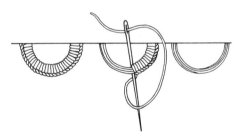

Figure 8

Marking the button position

After completing the button-holes, lay the garment on a flat surface and pin it together as it will be worn. Carefully pass a pin through the end of the button-hole nearest the edge, into the fabric underneath. Having established the button mark, repin more firmly. You can use a sharp pencil to do this but beware of mismarking on light fabrics.

Shanks

A shank is a small stalk that helps the button to move around and sit without strain on top of the button-hole, particularly with thicker fabrics.

Sewing on buttons by machine (Figure 9)

Note Use *two-holed* buttons only when sewing buttons on by machine.

1 Set up the machine with the special button-sewing foot (if the machine is supplied with one) or continue to use the normal zig zag sewing foot. Adjust the stitch length to 0.

2 Position the button and lower the foot to hold it in place. Set the zig zag width to fit between the two holes. Use the hand-wheel to test the stitch width and make a trial stitch. The needle will snap dangerously if you use the electric foot pedal.

3 Once the correct stitch width is established, proceed to sew the button on as normal. Approximately six stitches will hold the button secure.

4 Finish off the threads by pulling the needle thread through to the back of the work and knotting the two threads together.

5 If a shank is required, lay a matchstick between the holes and machine stitch over it.

Sewing on buttons by hand (Figure 10)

1 Thread your needle with a double length of thread. Use button-hole twist or linen thread for extra strength.

2 Take a tiny stitch with the knot on the *right* side of the garment. It will be hidden by the button.

3 Stitch the button into position. See Figure 10 for ways of tackling two- or four-hole buttons and shanks.

4 Make a shank by stitching over a matchstick. Wind the thread around the stalk for extra strength.

5 Finish off with tiny back-stitches on the wrong side of the garment.

Figure 9

Figure 10

17

Hooks and eyes (Figure 11)

This is the commonest kind of fastening used on waistbands and at necklines to hold the zip closure securely. Metal hooks and eyes are sold in a variety of sizes with either round or straight eyes. It is advisable to choose the larger heavier size for waistbands or areas of heavy strain.

1   The fastening should be invisible from the right side when closed so do not position the hook too close to the edge. Stitch into place with either a simple over-stitch or button-hole stitch, taking care that your stitches don't show on the right side of the garment.

2   Slip a pin into the fabric beneath the hook, placing the pin to correspond with the top of the hook to ensure a secure fastening. Place the hook over the pin if it is a straight eye or position the round eye with the top of the curve over the pin. Stitch to hold as before.

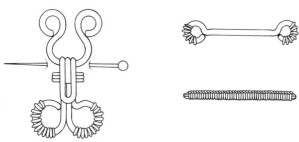

Figure 11

ALTERNATIVE EYE

The bulk of a metal hook and eye might spoil a lighter garment. To reduce this try a hand-sewn eye.

Using the method described for hand-stitched loop button-holes on p. 15, make a tiny bar with three or four over stitches and button-hole stitch around all of them.

CORD HOOKS AND EYES

These decorative hooks and eyes are called frogs, and are designed to be shown on the front of the garment. A good haberdashery department will have many designs of frogs, some of which can be very elaborate. They look effective as fastenings for heavier garments like coats, capes and furs.

1 Position them on the garment, remembering that the two edges of the garment underneath the frog must butt together and not gape.

2 Slip-stitch firmly on to the garment around the curls in a matching thread.

Press studs or snap fasteners (Figure 12)

Another method of making a neat closure for openings is to use press studs. These handy little items come in a variety of sizes and finishes including clear plastic for extra light or sheer fabrics.

1 Position the ball-shaped disc just inside the seam edge, to be invisible on the outside when closed. Stitch in place with an over-casting or button-hole stitch through each hole. Don't let your stitches show through to the right side.

2 To position the second disc accurately rub French chalk on the ball which will mark the correct place on the fabric underneath when pressed against it. Alternatively, slip a pin through the centre hole of the ball to pierce the under fabric. Stitch into place as before.

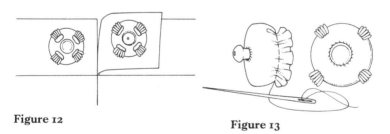

Figure 12

Figure 13

COVERED PRESS STUDS (Figure 13)

If you find the look of press studs unattractive, it is possible to conceal them. This method will give a couture finish to clothes. But be warned—it is finicky to do!

1 Cut out two circles of light fabric large enough in circumference to cover both sides of each disc. Use the garment fabric if light enough or a lining silk in a matching shade.

2 Cut a tiny hole in each centre for the ball and cup. Neaten around the edge with tiny button-hole stitches.

3 Gather the outer edges of the circle with a running stitch and tighten around each stud.

4 Stitch studs into position as described.

19

The popularity of fashions based on tough work clothes has made the humble metal stud a design feature in its own right. It is possible to decorate garments entirely with personalized patterns of studs, reminiscent of the old pearly kings and queens. A form of folk art has sprung up around the decorative uses of metal studs. Kits containing a hole puncher and studs with full instructions on how to use them are widely available at haberdashery counters. Do investigate using stud closure on appropriate items of your dressmaking; it can add a very professional finish.

Nylon tape fastening (Figure 14)

This arrival on the 'notions' dressmaking scene is marvellously adaptable. It is a boon for those, young and old, who have difficulty using the other more conventional methods of fastening their clothes. It takes the form of two tapes designed to stick together. One tape has a forest of tiny plastic hooks on one side that attach themselves into furry nylon filament on the other tape. It comes in many colours and is sold by the metre, which enables the dressmaker to cut and use as much or as little as required.

1   The tape must be invisible when closed, so position the loopy side of the tape away from the seam edge. Slip-stitch it into place or machine around the tape if extra strength is required and visible stitching lines don't matter.

2   Pin-mark the exact position of the second tape piece with the fuzzy surface, opposite the first tape. Sew it into place as described in 1.

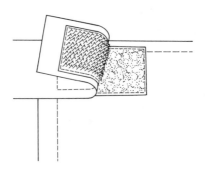

Figure 14

Zips

When putting in a zip you will achieve the best results only if you buy the right zip for the job. Make sure the zipper weight is compatible with the garment fabric. Too light or too heavy a zip will cause tensions with the seam and break the zip or tear the seam. The range of zips is enormous, they are made in lengths from 10 cm (4 in) to 56 cm (22 in) and in colours to match or tone with your fabric.

TYPES OF ZIPS

Nylon zips   For lightweight and sheer fabrics—dresses and skirts.

Metal zips   These are general-purpose zips for skirts and dresses. The coloured metal teeth are strong enough for daily wear and compatible with most weights of fabric.

Open-ended zips   These are only for use on jackets and coats. They come in a variety of weights from light metal zips for cardigans to big chunky zips for fur coats and other heavy garments.

Concealed zips   These are specially constructed zips which are completely invisible when closed; a neat seam line is all that can be seen.

Trouser zips   These are heavy-duty zips with plain metal teeth and an extra strong lock on the slider.

Jeans zips   These are really strong for the rough tough wear that denim jeans tend to be given.

BASIC METHODS FOR MACHINING ZIPS

Method 1 (Figure 15)

1   Fit your machine with the special zipper or cording foot which is designed to allow the needle to sew very close to the zipper teeth.
2   Position the needle to the left side, and having pressed the seam flat turn the zip over and place it with the tab at the top of the opening. Pin to hold and machine as close to the teeth as the zip will allow. Remember to start and finish with reverse stitches to strengthen. Run the slider down to check the freedom of movement.

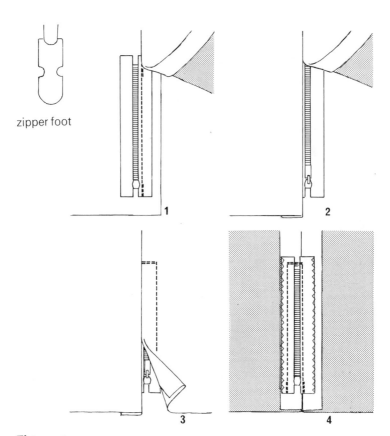

zipper foot

Figure 15

3 Turn the zip right side upward. This will conceal the stitching.
4 Move the needle over to the right side of the foot for this next step. Fold over the right side of the seam opening and butt the two seam edges together. Pin into position and machine stitch 6 mm ($\frac{1}{4}$ in) from the teeth, working on the right side of the fabric. Turn the corner at the base of the zip and machine twice across the bottom for strength.
5 Another line of stitching around the edge of the zip tape attaching it to the seam allowance will also add strength.

22

Method 2 (Figure 16)

1 Loosely tack the opening of the seam together and press flat.

2 Lay the garment on a flat surface whilst positioning the zip with its tabs butting to the top edge of the opening. Roll the zip down the seam with its teeth centred *exactly* over the seam opening. Pin to hold.

3 Position the needle to the right of the foot and machine round the zip 6 mm ($\frac{1}{4}$ in) from the teeth, working on the right side.

4 Finish inside as **5** in *Method 1*.

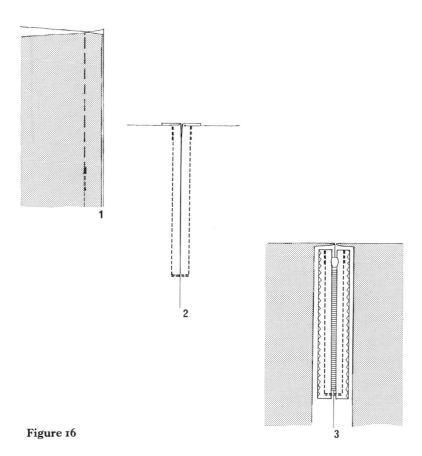

Figure 16

CONCEALED ZIPS (Figure 17)

It is easier to tackle this zip method *before* stitching the whole seam together.

1 Position the left side of the open zip face down on the left-hand piece of fabric. Pin to hold.

2 Use either the zipper/cording foot or a foot specifically designed for stitching concealed zips. Adjust the needle to be able to stitch right against the zipper teeth.

3 Roll the curved zipper teeth away from the needle and stitch down the tape. It is vital that the machine stitch lies right against the zipper teeth.

4 Close the zip and position it *exactly* over the seam line on the right-hand piece of fabric. Pin to hold.

5 Open the zipper and rolling away the teeth from the needle as before, stitch into place.

6 Close the zipper and stitch the remaining seam as usual.

7 For extra strength stitch the zipper tapes to the seam allowance.

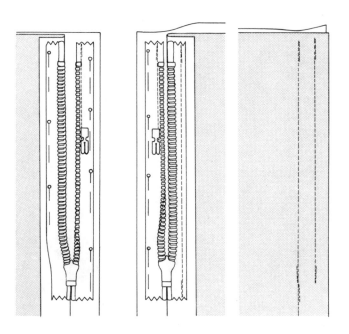

Figure 17

Quick tip (Figure 18)

This tip will enable you to use suitable second-hand zips from your own hoard of useful trimmings, or shorten new zips if required.

1 Decide on the new length for the zip and pin-mark.

2 Cut away a strip of tape from the bottom end of the zip.

3 Place the strip across the zip just below the new mark and machine stitch around the strip. Take care with the machine needle in the zipper teeth, use the hand wheel to guide through the teeth. The strip acts as a stop to the slider.

4 Trim away the unwanted zip and proceed to use the zip as normal.

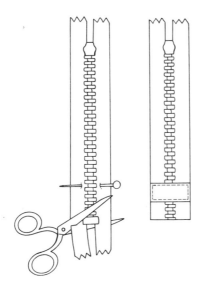

Figure 18

FLY-FRONT TROUSER ZIPS (Figure 19)

One of the most regular items in a busy family's mending schedule is the replacement of trouser zips. It is really worthwhile learning to do this properly as the economics of a new zip against new trousers or professional mending are obvious! It looks a daunting task with many layers and flaps to unpick and replace correctly. Follow these instructions, take it slowly and practice will make perfect. These drawings are for a man's trouser zip, so the top flap will be on the LEFT. Reverse side for a woman.

1 Tack the zip into position under the edge of the underflap on the right-hand side.

2 On the outside of the trousers tack the left-hand overflap into place to cover the zip.

3 On the inside of the trousers, position the free zipper tape on the overflap and machine in place as close to the teeth as possible. Take care to sew the zip only to the overlay, not the garment underneath. Two rows of stitching gives extra strength.

4 Tack the overlap to the trouser body.

5 Construct the fly as shown and machine to the underflap edge. Again take care to stitch only to the underflap.

6 Remove tacking from the outside of the trouser (2).

7 Open the zip and machine the zip tape tacked to the underflap. Sew from the outside stitching close to the teeth. Make sure all the layers of fly and underflap are sewn together.

8 The final stage is to machine the overlap into place. As the stitching is visible from the front, take care to make it straight with a good curve into the seam line.

9 A bar tack is worked at the base of the overlap stitching at the seam join. This can either be done with a machine satin stitch or by hand.

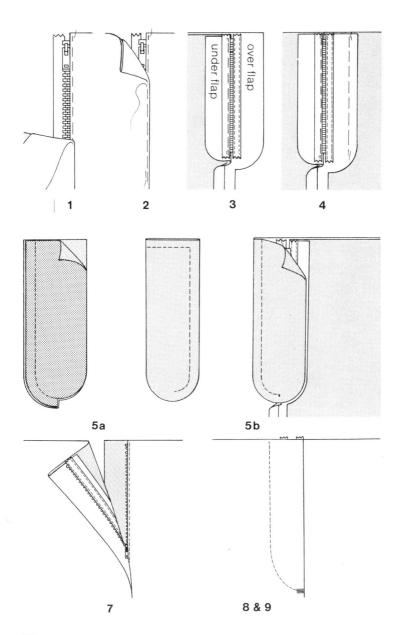

1   **2**   **3**   **4**

over flap

under flap

5a   **5b**

7   **8 & 9**

Figure 19

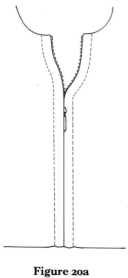

Figure 20a

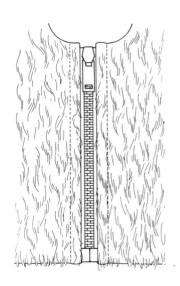

Figure 20b

OPEN-ENDED ZIPS (Figure 20)

There are two ways of stitching this kind of zip. The deciding factor is usually the garment fabric. Open-ended zips require to be free running and cannot afford to catch woolly fibres in the teeth. Therefore it is wiser to set the zipper teeth away from woolly and furry materials. Two ways of sewing in the zips, are illustrated. The basic method is the same as Method 2 at the beginning of this section, or setting the fabric away from the zipper teeth. Linings can be slip stitched into place just over the edge of the zipper tape for neatness.

28

Belts

It is not necessary to pay a high price for a good belt, because all the techniques and equipment for making them are available to the home dressmaker. Two basic methods of making belts are described; they are adaptable to every kind of material. Experiment for yourself with soft tie belts or stiff buckled belts to match or contrast with your outfit. Try different sizes, textures, buckles, ties, tassels, ribbons, cords, leather or suede; this list is endless. Enjoy this extension of your dressmaking skills and add the finishing touch of an individually designed belt.

TIE BELTS

The first method is best for heavier thicker material that does not turn easily, while the second way is ideal for light slippery materials. Cut a length of fabric the length and width you require, with seam and hem allowance. You may need to join pieces together to achieve the length.

Fold-and-stitch method (Figure 21)

1 Prepare your fabric with your iron as illustrated. Mitre the corners if necessary.
2 Top-stitch around the edges. Several rows of stitching can be done for a decorative effect.
3 Press.
Use this method to make belt loops. See page 62.

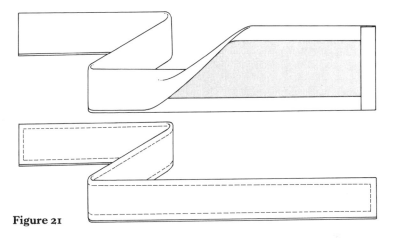

Figure 21

Turn-through method (Figure 22)

By making the 'turning-through gap' in the middle of a self-fabric belt, the belt ends can be machined neatly to finish with the seam either at the bottom or in the middle as shown in Figure 22. Use a fat wooden knitting needle to help turn through.

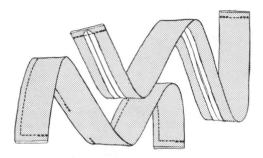

Figure 22

STIFF BELTS

Very good belt-making kits can be bought at haberdashery counters. The kits usually include buckle moulds to cover, stiffening for the belt body and eyelet punches to make the holes. When making the body of the belt, the width of the buckle bar determines the width of the finished belt. Cut a length of fabric to encompass your waist plus at least 15 cm (6 in) overlap. The width of the belt fabric must be double the buckle bar width—don't forget seam allowance 12 mm ($\frac{1}{2}$ in) all the way round. Now follow the fold-and-stitch method, but use a stiff iron-on interfacing or belt backing before folding over to stitch. Trim the interfacing to the fold lines to save bulk. Attach buckle and eyelets as instructed in the kit.

Chapter 2
Perfect hems

Some dressmakers find the prospect of turning up a hem nerve-racking. They invest in complicated aids to help achieve a perfectly level hem. All that is needed is a little planning and your usual dressmaking equipment.

The first, most important, step for trouble-free hems is to have altered your paper pattern to an approximately correct overall length BEFORE cutting out your material. By cutting out your garment accurately you will avoid pinning up very deep and wasteful hem allowances. The average hem on skirts is 5 cm (2 in) and in other places, such as trouser bottoms, jackets and sleeves it is 2.5 cm (1 in). This can vary with different fabrics and designs of garment. Do remember that the trouble that you take in preparing the hem will show one hundredfold in the professional appearance of your project.

Preparation

Step 1   Try on the garment to be hemmed. Remember to wear the correct lingerie and shoes for this final fitting, as this will affect your decisions about the length of the garment. Study yourself in a mirror, consider the current fashion lengths and your own body proportions in relation to the design of the garment. Pin up the hem just at the front to a height you like and keep adjusting this until you are satisfied with the overall look.

Here are several ways in which you can mark that final length right around your hem:

1   Request some assistance! Ask your volunteer to measure to the edge of the correct hem level upwards from the floor with a long ruler or a straight piece of wood. Mark the hem edge on the ruler or wood with a pencil. Unpin the garment back to its original

state and your helper can then mark the hem level with pins or tailor's chalk right around. Now pin up the hem to this level and check in your mirror that the complete hem hangs straight and level. Don't worry that the hem allowance underneath might be uneven, that is soon corrected – the outside appearance is more important.

2   The approach to hem levelling described in **1** is the time-honoured method but it is possible to level a hem accurately by yourself. Having found the chosen length in front of the mirror, stand beside your dining-room table and mark with chalk or pins the point at which the table edge rests against your hip. Turn slowly round, marking this at intervals (Figure 23a). Remove the garment and measure down from the table mark to the hem level, continue to measure down from the table mark all around the garment.

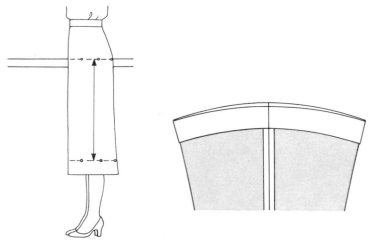

Figure 23a   **Figure 23b**

3   Finally, there is a quickie method! If you already know the depth of the finished hem, pin up the allowance right round the garment. Lay the garment on a flat surface with the two *side seams* together. The hem will be laid out in a semi-circle in front of you and any unevenness will be easy to see (Figure 23b).

Step 2   Having established the hem level round your garment, it is easy to lose the hemline as pins tend to drop out, or chalk marks fade. Lightly press the edge into place with your iron. This will save tacking round the hem and will preserve the hemline through the next processes. Continue working at the ironing board for the next stage in hem preparation, which is to trim the hem allowance to an even amount. Slip the skirt over the end of the ironing board as this enables you to see your area of work easily. Your paper pattern recommends the correct depth of hem, but if your hem allowance is less than this, then find the shortest depth of hem allowance on your garment. Measure from your newly pressed edge to this depth of allowance, mark it all round with pins or chalk and trim away the rest to match.

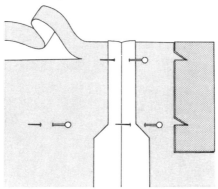

Figure 23c

Quick tip Make a hem depth gauge from a small piece of card or paper as illustrated (Figure 23c).

Step 3 You must now neaten the hem edge before finally stitching it into place. Use whichever seam neatening process you have already used on the rest of your project.

Step 4 To reduce ugly bulges in your smooth hemline, it may be necessary to trim the seam allowance as shown (Figure 23c).

Step 5 At last you have a level, even and neatened hem allowance to complete your stitching on. Pin the hem allowance back into place. If you have any surplus between the hem allowance and the outer garment, take small tucks in the hem allowance where the surplus falls naturally, usually near the side seams. Should there be a considerable amount of surplus read the section on circular skirts (p. 38).

Study the following methods for both machine and hand stitching and decide which you will use. Most garments look better with hand-stitched hems as they are—if well done—invisible. But machine-sewn hems that are designed to show are increasingly suggested in paper pattern designs.

Machine-stitched hems

1   Blind hem (Figure 24)

The stitch for this type of hem is done with a special blind-hemmer foot which is not essential but aids accuracy. If this foot is not available use your normal zig zag foot. Fold the hem as shown and press lightly to hold. Set the machine to the stitch illustrated, position the hem under the foot, to start just after a seam. The zig zag stitch must only catch a few threads of the top fabric. Heavier fabrics, particularly household furnishings, show less mark. Press well after sewing.

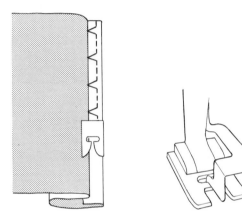

Figure 24

2   Top-stitched hems (Figure 25)

These narrow top-stitched hems are ideal for knits and cotton fabrics. Trim the hem to 16 mm ($\frac{5}{8}$ in) and finish the bottom edge either by zig zag stitch or by turning under 6 mm ($\frac{1}{4}$ in). Press hem allowance into place and proceed to stitch as illustrated.

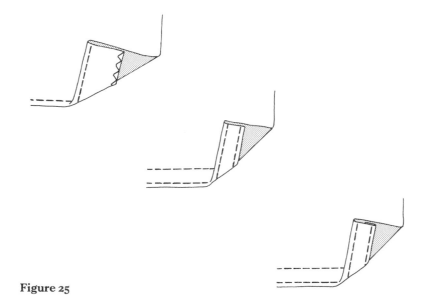

Figure 25

3 TAILOR'S HEM (Figure 26)

This method is particularly good for very heavy fabrics such as wool coating, as it reduces bulk in the hem area. Prepare the hem as before, then cut bias strips from a light fabric such as lining silk, to further reduce bulk, and stitch them together to form a strip long enough for the entire hem. Place the allowance edge and the binding right sides together and machine. Fold the bias strip over to enclose the raw edges and machine again. Hand slip-stitch to the garment as shown. See hand-stitched hems for advice on this. Press the hem edge only to finish off.

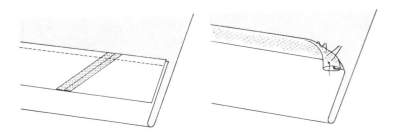

Figure 26

4   Bias-strip hem (Figure 27)

The procedure is the same as above except the raw hem allowance edge is not sealed inside the bias strip by a second row of machine stitching. Slip-stitch as shown, directly over the bias edge into the fabric not 3 mm ($\frac{1}{4}$ in) underneath the hem allowance edge as advised elsewhere.

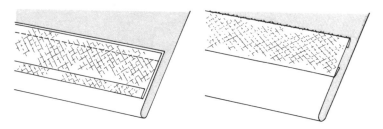

Figure 27

5   False hem

This hem finish uses the same method as the bias-strip hem (**4**), but the bias strip is cut deep enough to become the actual hem allowance. It is an ideal way to rescue garments that are too short! Level the hemline and trim to an even 12 mm ($\frac{1}{2}$ in) allowance all round, now proceed as in **4**, but position the seam between bias strip and garment edge just inside the wrong side of the garment. Press the hem edge only to finish off.

Hand-stitched hems

As mentioned earlier in this chapter the majority of hems are stitched by hand. This is simply because on most fabrics and designs an invisible hem looks better. The human hand is still better at picking up tiny threads than the domestic sewing machine. Please remember that for an extra professional smooth stitched hem, roll the top edge of the hem allowance back approximately 3 mm ($\frac{1}{8}$ in) and stitch below the edge. This prevents the stitching pressing the blunt edge of the fabric into the outer fabric. NEVER press this top edge, but allow it to float free from the garment.

BLINDSTITCH (Figure 28)

This is the best all-purpose stitch for hemming. Start by concealing the knot under a seam allowance and back-stitch a couple of
tiny stitches for strength. Roll the hem allowance down and working from right to left slip the needle into the garment, taking care
to only pick up one or possibly two threads. Now slide the needle
into the hem allowance a little further on than your first stitch.
Take up a larger stitch here as it will not be seen from the outside.
Proceed around the hem. You will find your stitches will establish
a rhythm and the whole task becomes very restful.

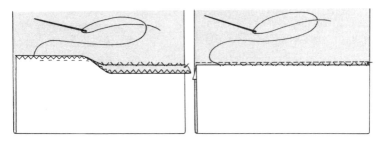

Figure 28   **Figure 29**

SLIP-STITCH (Figure 29)

This is another useful hand stitch which can be used on some types
of hem and other areas needing hand sewing to catch and secure.
Begin by concealing the knot and then do a couple of tiny back-
stitches to hold. Insert the needle into hem allowance and take
a small stitch, now pick up a thread of the garment at an angle
from your first stitch. Reinsert the needle into the fold and continue with stitching.

Quick tip (Figure 29)

For extra invisible slip-stitching, use the line of machine stitching
if one lies underneath, as with bound hems and facings. Pick up
every second machine stitch instead of a fabric thread and it
becomes easy to make hidden even slip-stitches.

Problem hems

FULL AND CIRCULAR SKIRTS (Figure 30)

It helps to hang up, overnight, garments with flared, circular or bias-cut skirts *before* beginning to prepare the hem level. The fabric will drop to its own level and this unevenness can be corrected when you pin up the hem the following day.

1 Find the hem level using method **1** or **2** (pp. 31–2). Don't worry if your very full skirt seems constantly to change levels; even if you have made it mathematically level the movement of your body disturbs the hang. Nothing can really be done about this; it is the nature of the skirt design.

2 Neaten the hem edge appropriately and pin the hem allowance back into place to gauge just how much surplus there is. Tack a line of gathering stitches through the worst areas just below the hem allowance edge. On very full skirts it is quicker to machine stitch a gathering line (longest stitch possible on your machine) around the hem.

3 Now begin to pin your extra-full hem allowance into position, drawing up the gathering thread to reduce the surplus. Press with your iron when all the hem allowance is evenly distributed. If your fabric shrinks, use a damp cloth at this point to steam shrink the hem allowance even further.

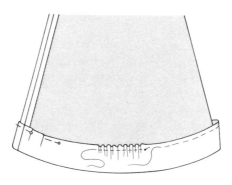

Figure 30

Quick tip

This method of running a gathering thread round hem edges works very well with curved hems such as on shirt tails (see Figure 31).

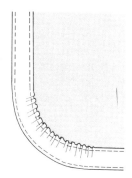

Figure 31

Leather and vinyls

The best way to tackle hems for these materials is not by sewing! The glue pot is the answer here. You will have learnt by the time you reach the hemming and finishing processes when working with leather and vinyl that they show every mark and mistake. *Extra* care is needed in preparation.

TO LEVEL THE HEM

Proceed as usual, but instead of pinning the hem in place use paper clips or hair clips. Once you are satisfied with the level, pound the hem edge with a heavy wooden block (not over the clips) to impress the hem edge. Trim away the hem allowance to approximately 5 cm (2 in) for a straight hem. Curved hemlines require a narrower hem allowance 2.5 cm (1 in) to 12 mm ($\frac{1}{2}$ in).

TO REDUCE BULK (Figure 32)

The problem of bulk at seams on real leather garments is dealt with by 'shiving', the method shown in Figure 32. Using a razor slice diagonally through the seam allowance.

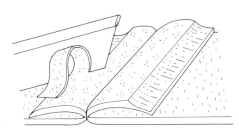

Figure 32

STICKING THE HEM

Use a rubber adhesive to hold the hem in place. Read and follow the product's instructions carefully. Keep the glue to within 6 mm ($\frac{1}{4}$ in) of the raw edge of the hem allowance to prevent the excess seeping over the top of the hem. Press by using your wooden block again to pound the hem.

PVC

The same problem exists for PVC as for leather. Follow the same procedures for levelling the hem and then use rubber adhesive and pound the finished hem. With lighter weight PVC there are alternative ways to hem. Experiment on scraps before choosing your final hem method.

TOP-STITCHING

Fold the 6 mm ($\frac{1}{4}$ in) hem allowance to the wrong side, use adhesive tape to hold in place while you machine stitch. To ease the plastic over the throat plate under the foot, sew over a layer of tissue paper or lightly coat the plate with machine oil. Set the machine for a straight or zig zag stitch. The larger the stitch the easier it will glide over the oily throat plate or tissue.

IRON-ON ADHESIVE TAPE

This is the simplest method of all! It is not suitable for leather unfortunately, as it requires a warm iron to melt the adhesive to stick the hem.

Quick tip

If all the gluing and 'shiving' and pounding with wooden blocks seems to be too heavy and troublesome for the design you're making, there is a simpler alternative—do nothing!

Leathers do not fray or stretch like ordinary materials, so nothing will happen if you merely trim the raw edge to the correct level and leave it. But this quickie method is really only recommended for the lighter leathers and suedes that make soft tops and skirts.

If you choose this method of finishing you could let your imagination run riot and devise lovely patterns to cut out on the hemline. A leather punch, which can be bought from specialist craft shops will give even greater scope for leather decoration. Illustrated are some ideas to give you inspiration (Figure 33).

Figure 33

Pleats

The main problem in hemming a pleated skirt is the bulk made by the numerous seams. Here are two ways that help.

Method 1 (Figure 34)

1 This method requires some forethought as the first stage begins at the start of garment construction. When stitching the skirt together finish all the seams about 20 cm (8 in) from the hem edge.

2 When the skirt is complete, level the hem, and neaten and stitch the hem, panel by panel.

3 Finally, machine the remainder of each seam together as shown. Neaten the seam edge as the fabric dictates, but angle the end of the seam as shown. This is necessary to help the hang of the pleat and reduce the bulk. Press.

41

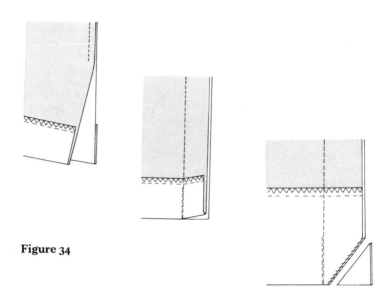

Figure 34

Method 2 (Figure 35)

Construct the skirt as normal, find the hem level and neaten the raw edge. When turning up the hem allowance clip the seam allowance as shown and proceed to hem stitch. Press.

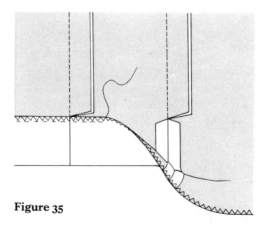

Figure 35

Quick tip

Lead weights are used by couture dressmakers to control light flyaway hemlines. These tiny discs of lead are sewn into small bags of the garment fabric and stitched, concealed in the hem allowance.

Sheer fabrics

The light floating quality of sheer fabrics is enhanced by the smallest hem possible.

MEASURING

It may help to hang the garment up overnight to allow it to drop before levelling the hem. This is especially true with garments cut on the bias. See method for levelling circular skirts on p. 38.

MACHINE-STITCHED HEMS (Figure 36a)

Rolled hem

A layer of tissue paper underneath the fabric will help control fine fabric. Gently tear away the tissue after stitching the hem. The foot illustrated is available for all types of machines. Set machine to a small straight stitch. Press the first very narrow fold in place round the hem then fold the work again in another narrow fold and sew a few stitches without threading the fabric into the roll. Now carefully thread your fabric into the roll and machine the hem. Hold the fabric taut and straight to feed into the roll. Practise this one!

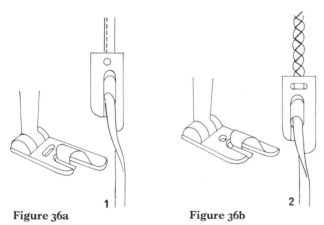

Figure 36a   **Figure 36b**

Shell hem (Figure 36b)

The foot for this hem looks the same as the hemmer, but is in fact for a swing-needle machine. It produces a delicate shell edge for lingerie and light, pretty hems. Use the same method as for rolled hems but set stitch settings for a medium zig zag. Different stitch widths alter the size of the shell pattern.

43

If you haven't the special foot described for rolled or shell hems don't despair. A perfectly acceptable machine-stitched hem can be sewn by using your normal foot and a medium-length straight-stitch setting. Turn the hem allowance under and machine stitch in the middle of the hem allowance. Add additional lines of stitching for decorative effect if you wish. Trim away excess hem allowance very close to the last row of stitching.

HAND-STITCHED HEMS

Both of these methods are painstaking and time-consuming, but the result is perfection. Use on the projects where your craftsmanship will create heirlooms.

Rolled hem (Figure 37a)

Trim the hem allowance to 6 mm ($\frac{1}{4}$ in). Fold in half to the wrong side. Take two vertical stitches picking up a thread in the garment and sliding the needle between stitches inside the fold. After every three groups of stitches gently tighten the thread and the narrow hem allowance will roll under.

Shell hem (Figure 37b)

Trim the hem allowance to 6 mm ($\frac{1}{4}$ in). Fold over twice to the wrong side and stitch as illustrated. Take three tiny running stitches in the fold of the hem allowance followed by one blanket stitch. Gently tighten the thread to create the shell effect.

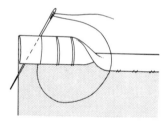

Figure 37a

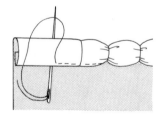

Figure 37b

Decorative hems

ELASTIC OR RIBBED EDGING

This easy and casual hem has grown from being used just on anorak jackets, to a whole range of fresh exciting design ideas. Haberdashery counters reflect this interest with new elastic trim-

mings, in lovely colours and textures. These range from fancy shir-
red elastics in various widths and colours to knitted ribbing. Of
course, if you are an accomplished knitter as well as dressmaker,
here is an area to combine your talents and knit collars and cuffs
and ribbing to co-ordinate with your project.

Measuring
To measure the amount of elastic/ribbing necessary to complete
the hem, gently stretch the trim around the portion of your body
that it will fit. It must be slightly stretched to fit snugly. Over-
stretching will cause strain and the trim will wear away much fas-
ter. Having found the right length cut away the excess
remembering to add 2.5 cm (1 in) seam allowance.

Stitching cuffs in place (Figure 38)

1 Taking a narrow seam allowance, stitch the two ends of the
band together.
2 Divide the circle into four sections on the elastic cuffs and
sleeve ends. Pin the circles of elastic and sleeve together, right sides
facing.
3 Set your machine to a medium zig zag stitch if you have one
or a long straight stitch if not. Machine slowly round stretching
the elastic to fit each quarter of the sleeve circle. There may still
be surplus sleeve to fit the trim, don't worry, just take tiny tucks
every so often and stitch over them. The tucks will disappear in
the general gathered look when finished.

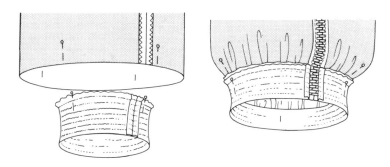

Figure 38

45

Stitching hems in place

1 Divide the hem and elastic trim into four quarters as described before.

2 Match the quarters together remembering to fold 12 mm ($\frac{1}{2}$ in) under to the wrong side at the opening. If the hem has no opening follow the method for cuffs.

3 Proceed to machine as described.

LETTUCE HEM (Figure 39a)

For the lettuce hem you will only need a simple zig zag stitch foot. This edge is best used on stretch jerseys and knits. Press a narrow hem 9 mm ($\frac{3}{8}$ in) in place and set the machine to a medium zig zag stitch. The secret of the rippled edge is to gently stretch the fabric as you stitch. Do test this hem first to get the right amount of stretch to stitch.

Figure 39a

Figure 39b

SCALLOPS AND SHAPED HEM EDGES

This section explains four different ways to make scallops and decorative shapes for hems and edges. Scallops are half circles set side by side. Other shapes can be used such as triangles and curly scrolls, which are just as attractive and easy to sew.

46

1   *Machine scallops* (Figure 39b)

This embroidery stitch is found only on fully automatic zig zag machines. The machine produces a continuous line of small satin-stitched scallops. This finish has many decorative uses from lingerie to table linen. Your own instruction book will show you how to set the machine. Use tissue paper or a strip of iron-on inter-facing under your fabric to help form the scallops. This is then removed.

2   *Machine satin stitch*

If you haven't an automatic machine or your design requires larger scallops or different shapes altogether, use the following method:

1   All zig zag machines sew a satin stitch. Set your machine to the widest width stitch and zero on the straight stitch guide.

2   Lightly draw the shapes on the fabric. Make sure the pattern repeats itself properly and is not cut off by seams or style lines.

3   Satin stitch is formed better if your fabric is laid over tissue paper or a small strip of iron-on interfacing. (Both will be removed after the first run of machining.) Experiment with controlling the width of the satin stitch by turning the stitch width control knob as you sew.

4   Repeat the satin stitch over the first run to clean the edge and form a neat solid row of stitching. One line rarely seems enough to give a finished appearance, but do experiment with your fabric before completing your stitching.

5   A thin cord can be fed under the foot on the second run of stitching. This will lie on the edge of the shape and give a crisp finish.

More tips and techniques for satin stitch sewing can be found in the section on appliqué in Chapter 4.

3   *Hand-sewn satin stitch*

The effects described above can be just as simply obtained by hand sewing. The decorative advantage of hand-sewn satin stitch is that you have a wider range of threads to stitch with, some being unsuit-able for use on a domestic sewing machine. Lovely designs can be sewn with wools, thick silks or even lurex threads.

a   Satin stitch is repeated over and over starting and finishing the thread immediately beside the previous stitch (Figure 40a). Be careful not to make too deep a stitch; 12 mm ($\frac{1}{2}$ in) is about the maximum.

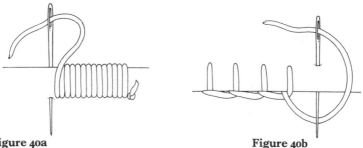

Figure 40a   **Figure 40b**

b Blanket stitch is good for heavy fabrics that fray easily. It looks lovely when done in contrasting silk or wool threads. Insert the needle approximately 6 mm ($\frac{1}{4}$ in) from the edge of the seam, draw the thread across and behind the needle, through and out of the fabric. Gently tighten the stitch to form a neat line along the seam edge (Figure 40b).

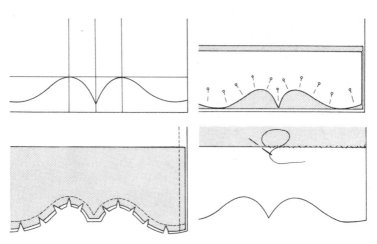

Figure 41

4 *Faced hems* (Figure 41). This method of making a shaped edge is rather heavy when finished, so it is wise to choose a strong fabric. Furnishing cotton is an ideal fabric, so this particular method is more suitable for home furnishings than a light dress.

a A paper pattern of the shape and size of your chosen hem must be drawn up first. Draw your shapes accurately on to paper positioning the shapes to their best advantage. Remember hem and seam allowance are to be included.

b Measure and cut a strip deep enough to cover the shapes plus approximately 5 cm (2 in).

c Lay the hem of your project on a flat surface and pin on the strip right sides together. Place the paper pattern on top and cut round the pattern through both layers of fabric.

d Carefully remove the paper pattern and machine around the shapes.

e Trim away the seam allowance in steps to reduce the bulk and clip into the corners and at regular intervals to help the hem to lie flat. Turn through and push the shapes into place with a plump knitting needle or point of scissors to ease out the corners. Roll the seam edge between your fingers to help it lie flat on the edge of the shape.

f Press well.

g Turn under the raw edge and slip-stitch it into place.

Iron-on adhesive tape

If all that has gone before in this chapter on hems does not answer your problem or just proves too much work, try the following method. The simplest and quickest way to secure a hemline is to use iron-on adhesive tape, so throw away your needle and thread and get out your iron! This double-sided adhesive tape comes in a variety of widths, the most useful being 2.5 cm (1 in) wide. But don't use it on fabrics that are difficult to apply heat to, such as velvets and sequin-embroidered fabric.

1 The instructions for hem levelling and preparation still apply.

2 Set your iron to a warm temperature, and slip the garment over the ironing board.

3 Position the tape under the hem allowance, below the top edge and lightly press to hold. Adjustment can be made at this point by easing the tape and fabric apart and repositioning and pressing.

4 When the entire hem is correctly positioned and stuck down, take a damp cloth and repress applying firm pressure to give a strong bond.

5 Leave to cool before touching to allow the glue time to set.

Quick tip

Use iron-on tape to mend falling hems quickly. Repeated steam pressing with a damp cloth will remove the adhesive when you have time to restitch the hem properly.

Chapter 3
Linings

To line or not to line: this is a controversial subject to a dressmaker. Until recently there would have been no question—clothes were lined. But with the soft, relaxed look predominating in fashion now, linings are rarely used except in very tailored suits and coats. There is no doubt that the addition of a silky shell inside heavier skirts and dresses gives the skin a more sympathetic surface to rest against. Linings also maintain the shape of garments thereby adding to their lifespan. But this strength can give an air of rigidity to the garment, which runs against current ideas of soft body-defining clothes. To sum up—whether to line or not depends on your choice of fabric and design; it can make or mar the finished look.

Choice of lining

The firmly woven silky fabrics used for lining come in many weights from crêpes to heavy satins. When choosing a lining always drape the top fabric over it and handle the two together. Always check the laundering instructions—disasters can happen when a washable garment is lined with a 'dry clean only' silk!

Banish the idea that all linings should be plain and functional. You can add great flair to a plain suit by lining the jacket with a lively patterned silk. A blouse to match the patterned jacket lining can lift a formally tailored outfit.

Lining pattern pieces

Your purchased pattern will give the appropriate pattern pieces for the lining if one is recommended. Make up the lining according to pattern instructions.

Important Don't attempt to line a garment made from a paper pattern that is designed and cut for stretch-knit fabric only. The nature of stretch fabric would be ruined with a lining.

If, however, you have decided to line your garment and there is no lining pattern, use the pattern pieces of the body of your design as given below.

JACKET OR COAT LINING

Use all the front and back body patterns and sleeve as well. Add an extra amount of fabric, about 5 cm (2 in), to the back body pattern at the centre back when cutting out. This is tucked into a pleat at the neck when stitched into the jacket or coat body and allows for ease of movement when the garment is worn.

SKIRT

Use the back and front skirt pieces. Cut the lining shorter by the length of the hem allowance for the skirt. Complicated styles with, for example, pleats are better lined with a simple straight skirt shape rather than attempting to follow the original design.

DRESS

Use the entire back and front dress pieces with sleeve if required. Cut the lining shorter by the length of the hem allowance of the dress. If the dress has a waist seam, cut and make the lining to match, sewing the lining together with the dress at the waist seam.

Sewing in the lining

Having cut out the lining, machine the pieces together to make a duplicate of the garment. The following instructions tell you how and when to sew it into the garment.

Remember All linings are sewn into a garment wrong sides together.

SKIRT

Machine the made-up lining into the skirt around the waist, before the waistband is stitched into place. Slip-stitch the lining into place around the zip.

DRESS

Machine the made-up lining around the neck and armholes before the facings or sleeves are sewn on. Slip-stitch around the zip. Hem the lining either by hand or machine.

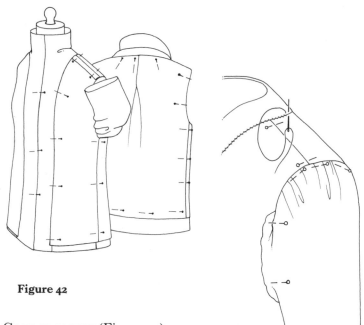

Figure 42

COAT OR JACKET (Figure 42)

The easiest way to fit the lining in place in a coat or jacket is with a dressmaker's dummy. Failing this, hang the garment on a padded coat hanger; it will give sufficient body to the shoulders. Suspend the hanger at a level that is comfortable for you to work at.

1 Turn the coat or jacket inside out and settle it on the dummy or hanger. Fasten buttons and zips and arrange the garment to hang correctly.

2 Slip on the body of the completed lining, pinning to hold it on the shoulders at the neck and sleeve head. Position and pin the lining and garment together at these seams: underarm, side seam at the hem, and front facing at the hem. If the lining sits well and shows no terrible faults, continue to pin lining around the outer edge of the garment facing and hem. Turn the lining under approximately 6 mm ($\frac{1}{4}$ in) as you go. **Remember** to pleat the lining at the back neck and ease the surplus in along the back hem.

3 Then slip on sleeve lining and pin the underarm seams. Match the sleeve head notch with the shoulder seam. You may find it easier to gather the sleeve head of the lining to take up the surplus fabric.

52

4 Repeat the pinning process around the armhole turning under the lining as you go.

5 Slip-stitch right around the pinned areas catching the lining to the garment.

6 If preferred leave the lining free at the hemline and catch the previously machined hem lining to the seam points. This will give the lining more freedom of movement.

Mounted lining (Figure 43)

This way of lining is quicker than the traditional method explained before. It gives more strength and body to a garment than a loose lining, which makes it ideal for clothes that receive hard wear. Skirts in particular benefit from this method. The technique is to cut the lining out with the garment and stitch the two layers together as one when constructing the garment. The disadvantage of this is obvious—nothing is hidden beneath it! Garments made in lace, chiffon or mohair will hold their shape better if mounted on a silk or very light cotton.

1 Cut out the fabric. Make all the necessary balance marks, remove the pattern and open up each of the body pieces.

2 Lay the lining out in a single layer and pin on the open fabric pieces and cut out.

3 Machine right round each pattern piece with a zig zag stitch to seal the two layers together.

4 Proceed to construct the garment as usual. It will take less time as the seam neatening and lining processes have already been done!

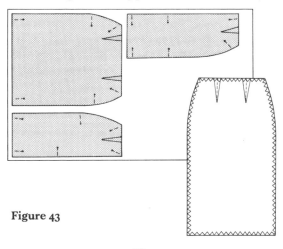

Figure 43

53

Chapter 4
Making it pretty

There are so many trimmings on the market that it would fill a separate book just to describe them. The best place to find out about the range available is a large haberdashery department.
Bear the following points in mind when buying trimmings.

1 Choose a trimming that complements your fabric weight. A light cotton garment would look odd with a heavy wool braid as would a heavy wool jacket trimmed with cotton bias binding.

2 Check the washing instructions! Make sure you have washable trimming on a washable garment.

3 If the colour you require isn't available, buy a neutral shade like cream or white in your chosen trim and dye it. Make sure you dry clean the garment as colour cannot be guaranteed fast with home dyeing.

Sewing on braids, ribbons and laces

This is really just a question of straightforward machining, but it requires a steady hand and eye to keep the stitching lines straight. It is important that the trim looks crisp and neatly stitched when finished or the effect can be ruined. Here are some tips:

1 Buy an extra 25 cm ($\frac{1}{4}$ yd) trim for testing.

2 Your stitching lines will be less obvious if you use finer thread—no 40 or no 30 are best.

3 Use small patches of double-sided iron-on adhesive tape to anchor the trim at strategic points before machining.

4 A straight or zig zag machine stitch can be used. Always test a scrap of trim on a small piece of fabric to find the right stitch.

5 A narrower foot for straight stitching is a real help; the normal foot width can drop off the edge of the trim and distort the stitching.

6 Unpicking the wrong stitching from trimming gets problematical, and a crisp finish gets that chewed string look very quickly. *Should* an accident happen use the following method to unpick and restitch (Figure 44):

a) Snip the bobbin thread stitch in the middle of the 'wobbly' area. Ease out the stitches with a pin, back to the good machining.

b) Snip and pull the needle thread through to the underneath and knot it together with the bobbin thread.

c) Now gently guide the machine needle into the base hole of the last stitch, lower the presser foot and restitch the 'wobbly' area.

d) Pull through the needle thread to knot with the bobbin thread at each end of the sewing.

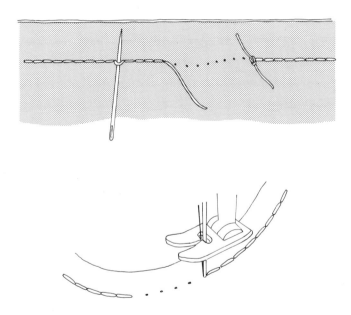

Figure 44

MITRING CORNERS (Figure 45)

1 First stitch the trim on the outside edge, carefully turning the corner as illustrated.

2 You will see that the surplus trim on the corner cannot lie flat. Fold this surplus in a neat diagonal fold and pin.

3 Now stitch the inside edge of the trim, repeat the manoeuvre to turn the corner.

4 Slip-stitch the folded mitre to hold in place.

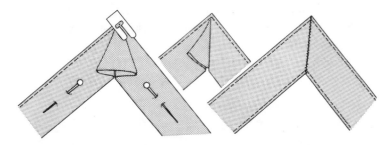

Figure 45

COPING WITH CURVES

1 Many trims respond to steam pressing and can be eased into shape on the ironing board before stitching on to your garment. Test a scrap of trim to find out.

2 If this fails use the method described for easing circular hems page 38. Run a gathering thread along the edge and press into shape.

Inserting pre-gathered lace and piping into seams
(Figure 46)

This is one of the most frequently used trimming techniques, especially in soft furnishings.

1 Set up your machine with the zipper or cording foot. Without this invaluable aid it is almost impossible to achieve a seam that does not show part of the backing of the lace or cord.

2 Position the lace or cord on the right side of the fabric and run a line of straight machine stitching to hold.

3 Place the facing or next fabric layer on top and stitch the seam as close as possible to the cord, or with lace, close to the taped edge.

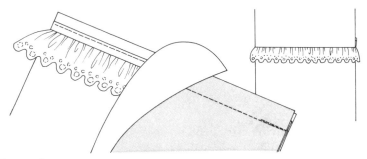

Figure 46

Bias binding

Use the method described for tailor's hems on page 35. Steam press to shape the binding for curves.

Bows (Figure 47)

Never tie a bow as you would your shoelace and stitch the result on your garment. It will look just like a shoelace! Decorative bows that have no function are constructed in layers to give a crisp finish.

1 If you are using the same fabric as your garment make a tube of fabric as shown in the section on belts, page 29.

2 Fold the tube in half and lay the ends in the middle. Pin to hold.

3 Lay a straight tube of fabric underneath this if you want ends to the bow.

4 Wrap a short length of tube around the middle of these two and slip-stitch into place.

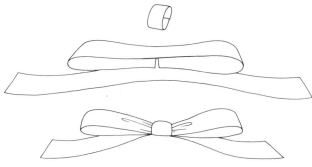

Figure 47

Appliqué

Bright, amusing pictures made in material can raise your garment or soft furnishing project from the ordinary to an original. Whether you use purchased appliqués or make your own, you will have fun sewing them.

PURCHASED APPLIQUÉS

When you are buying one of the many designs that are now sold, check the cleaning instructions for the appliqué. Look also at the finish of the edges. Most have a clean neat satin stitch which will only require hand over-stitching into place. A poorly finished edge will begin to look tatty after wear unless you stitch it securely in place either by machine zig zag or satin stitch.

MACHINE SATIN STITCH

For those of you with a swing-needle machine, the technique of appliqué work with satin stitch is well worth mastering, but it requires practice. Your own machine manual should have details of stitch settings and methods of sewing. Here are some basic techniques to help produce a good finish.

1 Use a small embroidery frame. This will hold the work taut and ease the sewing movements.
2 Lower the dog feed teeth if possible. (Some machines do not lower them, so check your machine manual.) These serrated teeth lie in the throat plate and guide the sewing away from the needle. This will give you complete freedom of stitching movement—not just forwards and backwards.
3 A backing of iron-on interfacing on the fabric really helps to keep the smooth sewing movements which are essential for even rows of satin stitch. It can be peeled off around the design afterwards.

Turning corners (Figure 48)
Finish the first line of satin stitch with the needle in the outer edge, lift the foot, turn the work to face the new line and lower the foot. Carefully sew over the original line at the corner then continue down the second line.

Curves
This is the basic technique for all curves. Stitch into the middle of the turn, use the inner edge hole of the last stitch as the pivot

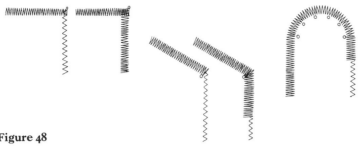

Figure 48

of the curve. Turning the hand-wheel to sew, stitch around the curve with each stitch beginning in the pivot hole. Turn the work fractionally with each stitch.

The fully automatic zig zag machine has a range of embroidery stitches which are also suitable for stitching appliqué. Experiment with some of these for variation.

HAND-STITCHED APPLIQUÉ

There are a variety of hand embroidery stitches that can be used to attach an appliqué design. In fact the stitch itself becomes part of the appliqué design, giving a wider scope for creativity than satin stitch.

1 *Slip stitch* For method see page 37.

2 *Chain stitch* Make a loop with a tiny stitch which is not pulled tight. Pass the needle through the fabric about 3 mm ($\frac{1}{8}$ in) further on and catch the loop under the needle as shown. Pull gently to lay the loop on the fabric and repeat for the next loop in the chain. (Figure 49a).

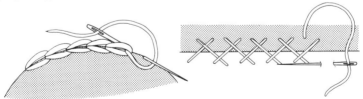

Figure 49a   **Figure 49b**

3 *Herring-bone stitch* This looks like an extended cross stitch and is worked from left to right taking small stitches above and below the appliqué edge. (Figure 49b).

4 *Blanket stitch* For method see page 48.

Chapter 5
Final touches

No garment, however beautifully made, will give the wearer pleasure if it is not comfortable to wear. These ideas will help your new outfit to stay comfortably in place and help you forget its presence.

Dress shields (Figure 50)

Light cotton dress shields are a great boon during warm weather—particularly if you rely on a fresh, clean appearance. They are expensive to buy, considering how little fabric and work is involved. Why not make your own? Choose a light but closely woven cotton and trace the pattern shape in Figure 50. Cut eight shapes for double shields suitable for sleeved garments. Cut four for sleeveless garments.

MAKING DOUBLE SHIELDS

Machine four pieces together along the armhole curve and trim the seam back to 3 mm ($\frac{1}{8}$ in). Fold the two top half-circles from either side over to meet each other, enclosing the seam. Set your machine to the widest zig zag stitch or a short straight stitch. Sew the two sides of each half-circle together, repeat for the other shield.

MAKING SINGLE SHIELDS

Machine two shields together along the armhole curve and trim the seam back to 3 mm ($\frac{1}{8}$ in). Turn the half-circles to enclose the seam and zig zag as described. Repeat for the other shield.

Lightly overstitch the two points of the shield to the armhole seam to hold in place. Tiny press studs would simplify removal for laundering if the garment is worn constantly.

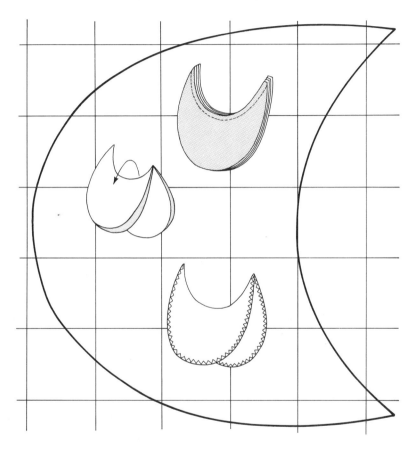

Figure 50

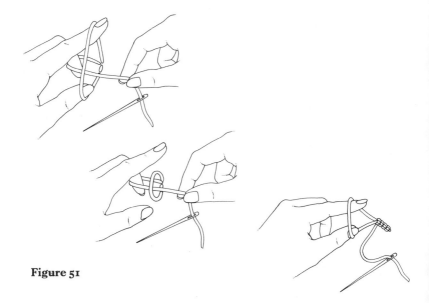

Figure 51

Belt loops

Designed to hold wandering belts in place, these can either be almost invisible (*Method 1*) or part of the design (*Method 2*).

METHOD 1 — HAND-KNOTTED LOOPS (Figure 51)

1 Using your sewing thread or matching button-hole twist, thread your needle with a long double thread and pass it through the seam at the waistline to the right side. Hide the knot under the seam allowance.

2 Take a tiny stitch to form a loop. Hold the loop in the left hand, catch the needle thread with the middle finger and draw the thread through the loop.

3 Slip the first loop off the fingers on to the thread to make a second loop. Tighten the first loop right down to the side seam.

4 Repeat the process as many times as necessary to make the right length of knotted cord needed to make a loop to fit your belt.

5 To finish off, repeat the looping procedure but this time draw the needle thread through the loop and tighten.

6 Lay the knotted cord down the side seam to find where to pass the needle through the side seam to the wrong side of the garment. Stitch to hold.

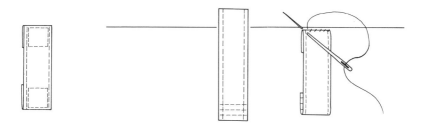

Figure 52a   **Figure 52b**

METHOD 2—FABRIC LOOPS (Figure 52)

1   Cut the fabric the width of the belt plus 2.5 cm (1 in) turning allowance, top and bottom.
2   Using the fold-and-stitch method shown on page 29, make the required number of strips.
3   Attach at the waistline either by top-stitching as shown (Figure 52a) or slip-stitching for the concealed method (Figure 52b).

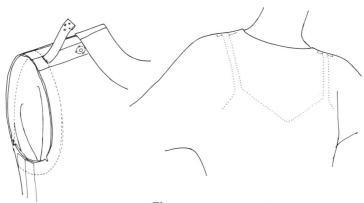

Figure 53

Strap loops (Figure 53)
Make use of your lingerie straps to hold loose tops in place.
1   Stitch one end of a small piece of ribbon 4 cm (1½ in) to the shoulder seam of your garment.
2   On the other end of the ribbon stitch one half of a press stud.
3   Stitch the other half of the press stud on to the shoulder area. Repeat for the other shoulder.
4   When you are dressed slip the ribbon under the lingerie straps and close the press stud.

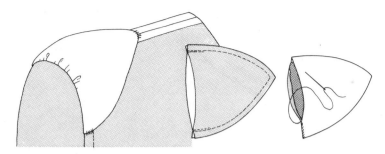

Figure 54

Shoulder pads (Figure 54)

These slim pads greatly improve the hang of coats and jackets when stitched into the sleeve head. In most cases the pads are stitched in and then concealed by lining. Should you wish to use pads in unlined garments here is the method of covering them.

1 Choose a light cotton or silky lining fabric to match or tone with the garment.

2 Cut out two shapes using the pad as a pattern. Don't forget to add a seam allowance all around the shape.

3 Stitch around the half-circle and trim away the seams to 3 mm ($\frac{1}{8}$ in). Turn the half-circles right side out.

4 Slip the pad into this pocket and stitch up the opening.

5 Position the pad to your satisfaction inside the garment. Use your mirror to see where the pad best suits you. If you place the pad too far into the sleeve head it will distort the hang of the sleeve.

6 Slip-stitch on to the armhole seams and at the shoulder seam. Don't stitch on to the actual garment as it will create an ugly ridge.